Press-out Paper Town

Illustrated by Francesca Di Chiara

Designed by Suzie Harrison

Written by Fiona Watt

Additional illustrations by Ian McNee

Hints and tips

1. **Carefully tear out** the page along the perforations before you start to make a model.

2. **Don't press out all the pieces in one go.** Press out each piece as you follow the step-by-step instructions.

3. **Press out** any windows and pop open the doors before putting the pieces together.

4. **If the pieces come apart** when you slot them together, just bend the tabs a little to secure them.

5. **Read the labels carefully** so that you know which is the outside and which is the inside of a building, and where you should fold each piece.

6. **You'll find lots of little white press-out pieces** on the last page. These are the stands for the figures.

Slot them together, like this.

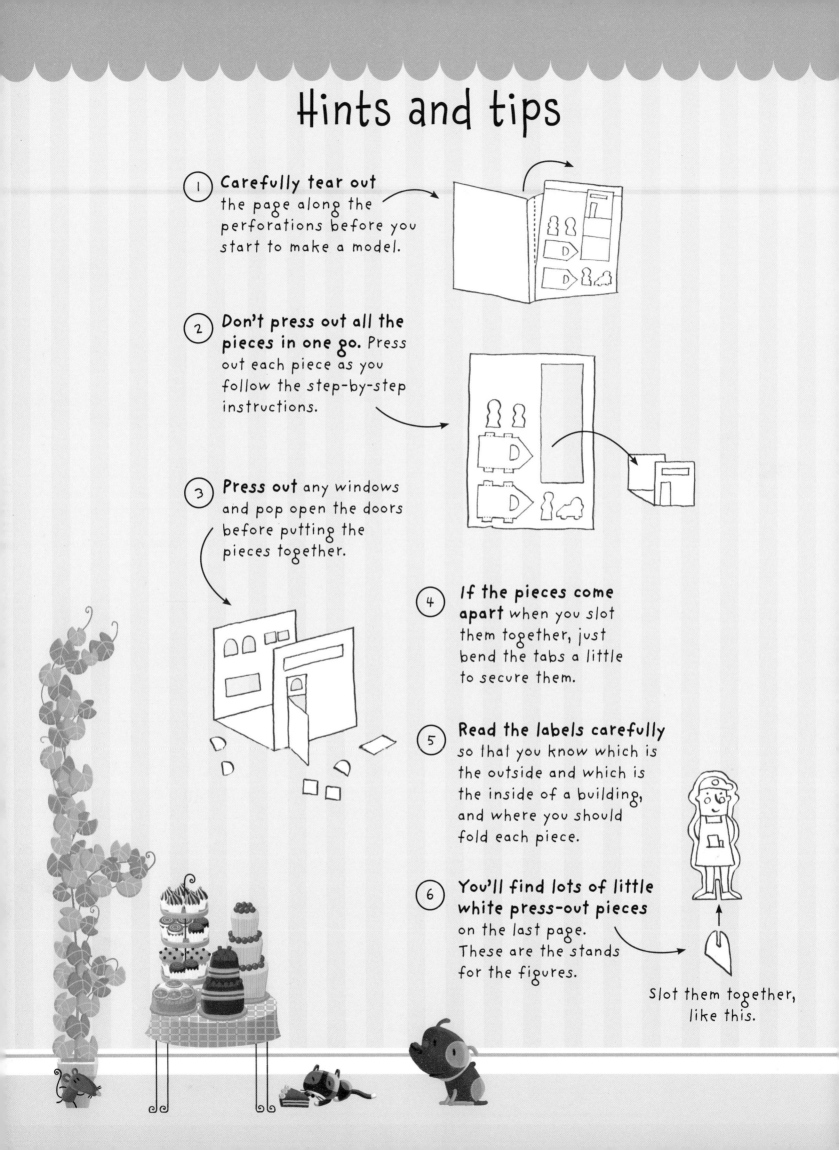

The greengrocer's

1. Press out the shop. Then, fold the walls down along the crease lines.

2. Stand the shop on its base. Press out the side walls, then slot them in like this.

The steps continue on the next page.

Mr. George the greengrocer

Greengrocer

Fold down here

Outside wall

Outside wall

The outside of the shop

The inside
of the shop

Inside wall

Inside wall

The greengrocer's continued

3. Press out the roof and fold it along the crease. Then, slot the roof onto the side walls of the shop.

4. Press out the stall for the front of the shop. Fold in both sides, then fold the top down along the two crease lines.

Stall

Fold here

Fold here

The roof

Fold here

5. Turn the page over to find this step.

Scott's sweet shop

1. Press out the roof and fold it along the crease. Put it to one side.

2. Press out the window awning, then fold the top and the sides along the crease lines.

The steps continue on the next page.

Fold here

The outside roof

Fold here

Fold here

Window awning

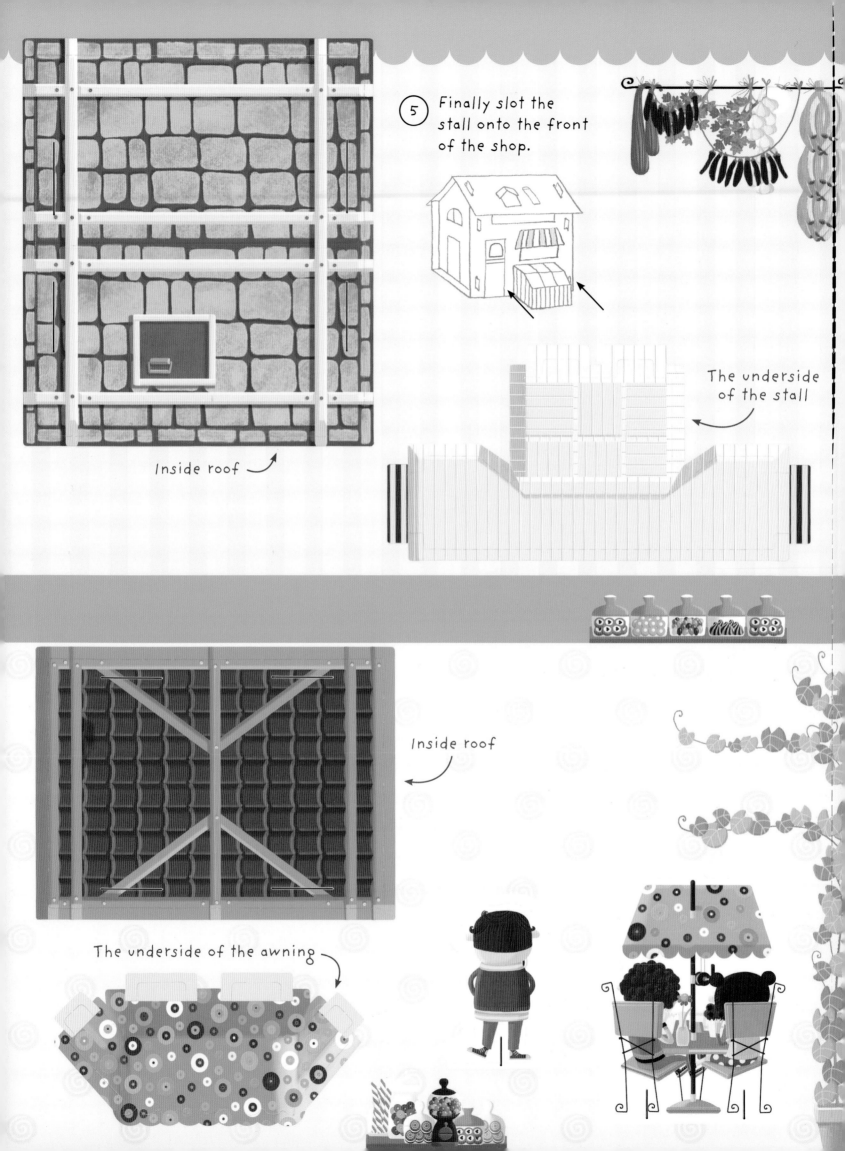

Inside roof

5 Finally slot the stall onto the front of the shop.

The underside of the stall

Inside roof

The underside of the awning

Scott's sweet shop continued

③ Press out the shop. Then, fold the walls down along the crease lines.

④ Stand the shop on its base. Press out the side walls, then slot them in so that the plants are on the outside.

⑤ Look on the back of this page for this step.

Outside wall

Outside wall

Mr. Scott sells ice cream outside his shop.

Mrs. Scott

Scott's sweet shop

Fold here

The outside of the shop

The inside of the shop

⑤ Slot the awning below the shop sign, then add the roof.

Inside wall

Inside wall

Flora's flower shop

1. Press out the shop. Fold the walls along the creases so that the pink walls are on the outside. Then, fold the walls around and slot the tabs into the end wall.

Slot the tabs in here.

2. Turn the shop upside down and fold the floor down. Push the tabs into the slots.

Flora the florist

3. Press out the roof and turn it over. Fold it back along the two creases, then slot the tabs into the roof. The shop name should be on the outside.

The roof

Fold here

Flora's flower shop

4. Turn the page over to find this step.

Fold the tabs here

The outside of the flower shop

Fold here

Fold here

Fold here

Fold here

Fold here

Fold here

Fold the tabs here

4) Fold down the large flap in the wall, to make a shelf. Then, slot the roof onto the shop.

Fold the flap down, like this.

The inside of the shop

The top of the roof

Carlo's café

1. Press out the café. Fold the walls along their creases so that the purple walls are on the outside. Fold the walls around, then slot the tabs into the end wall.

2. Turn the café upside down and fold the floor down. Fold the tabs and push them into the slots.

Side awning

Carlo

Fold the tabs here

3. Press out the roof. Fold the ends of the awning back.

Awning

The outside of the roof

4 and 5 Turn the page over to find these steps.

Fold here

Fold here

Café

Fold here

Fold here

Fold here

Fold the tabs here

4. Slot the roof onto the café. Then, slot the tabs of the awning into the walls.

5. Press out the side awning. Crease it along its folds, then slot it into the side wall.

Side awning

The inside of the café

The inside of the roof

The Town Hall

① Press out the Town Hall.
Then, fold the walls down
along the crease lines.

② Press out the door
surround. Fold it
along its crease
lines, then put it
to one side.

The steps continue
on the next page.

The outside of the Town Hall →

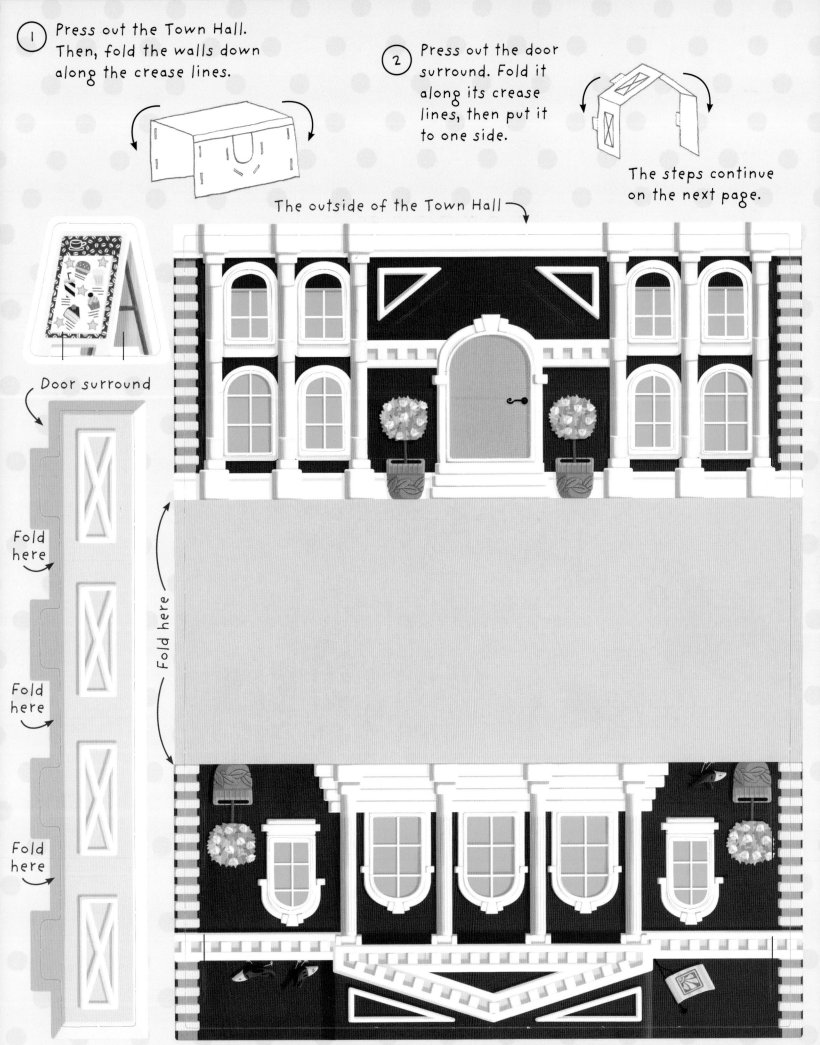

Door surround

Fold here

Fold here

Fold here

Fold here

Fold here

Inside the Town Hall

Display sign for a cake sale

Cake sale

The Town Hall continued

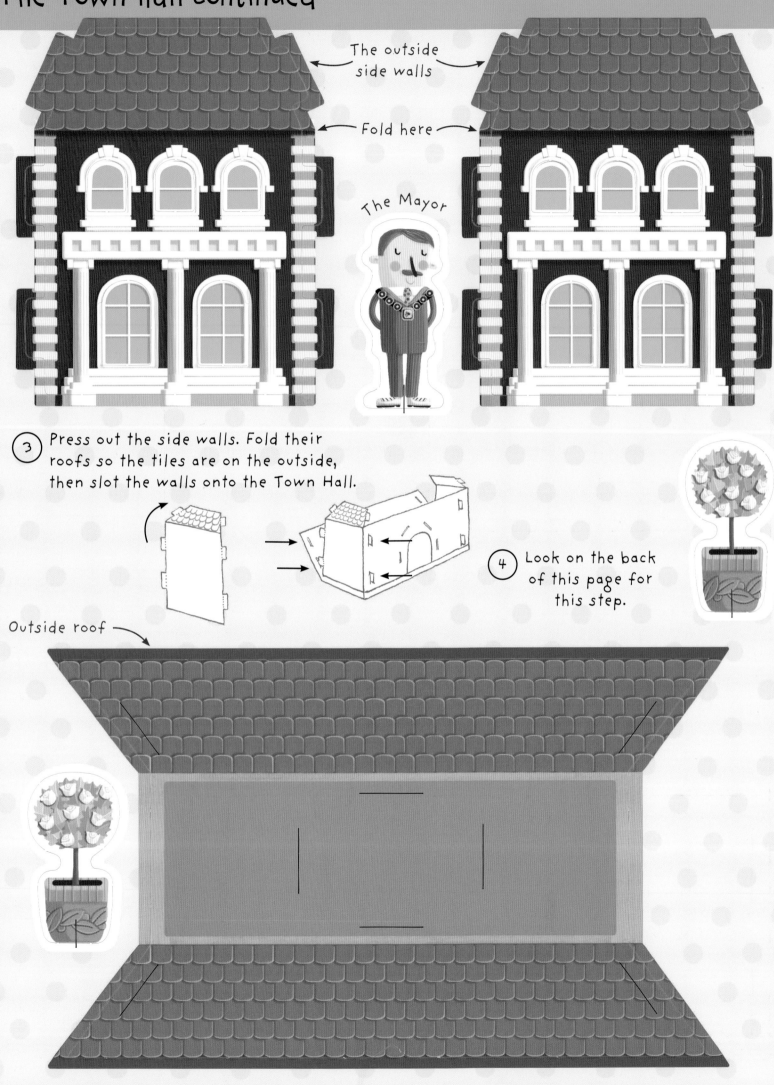

The outside side walls

Fold here

The Mayor

3 Press out the side walls. Fold their roofs so the tiles are on the outside, then slot the walls onto the Town Hall.

4 Look on the back of this page for this step.

Outside roof

The inside
walls

Fold
here →

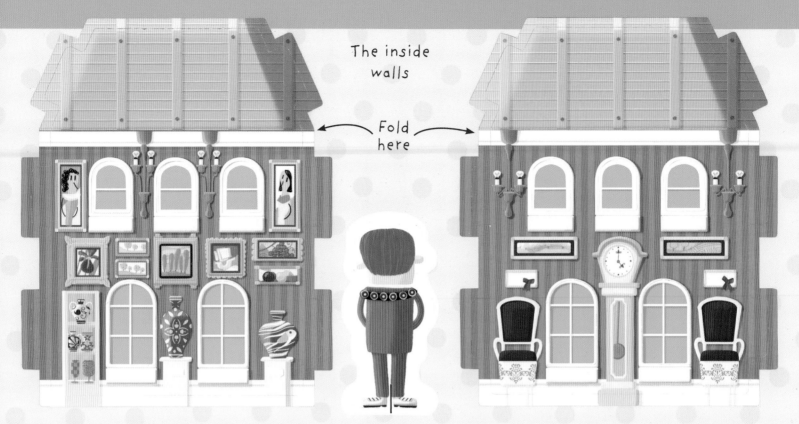

④ Press out the roof, then
fold it along the crease
lines. Slot the roof onto
the Town Hall. Then, slot
the door surround around
the door.

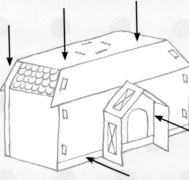

⑤ and ⑥
These steps are
on the next page.

Inside roof

Fold here ↷

Fold here ↷

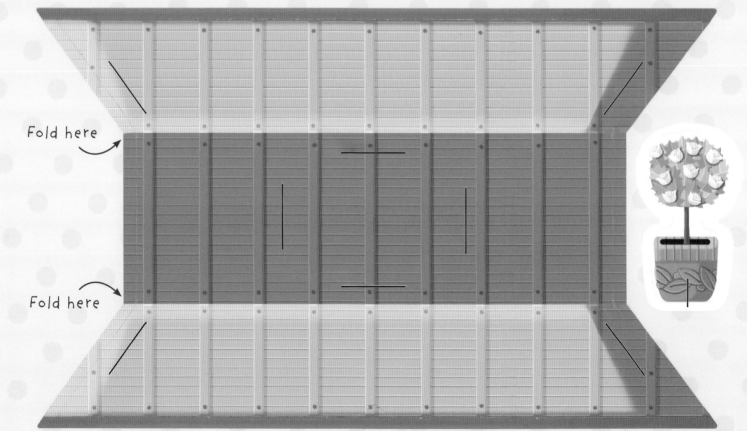

This side goes above the doorway.

The Town Hall
continued

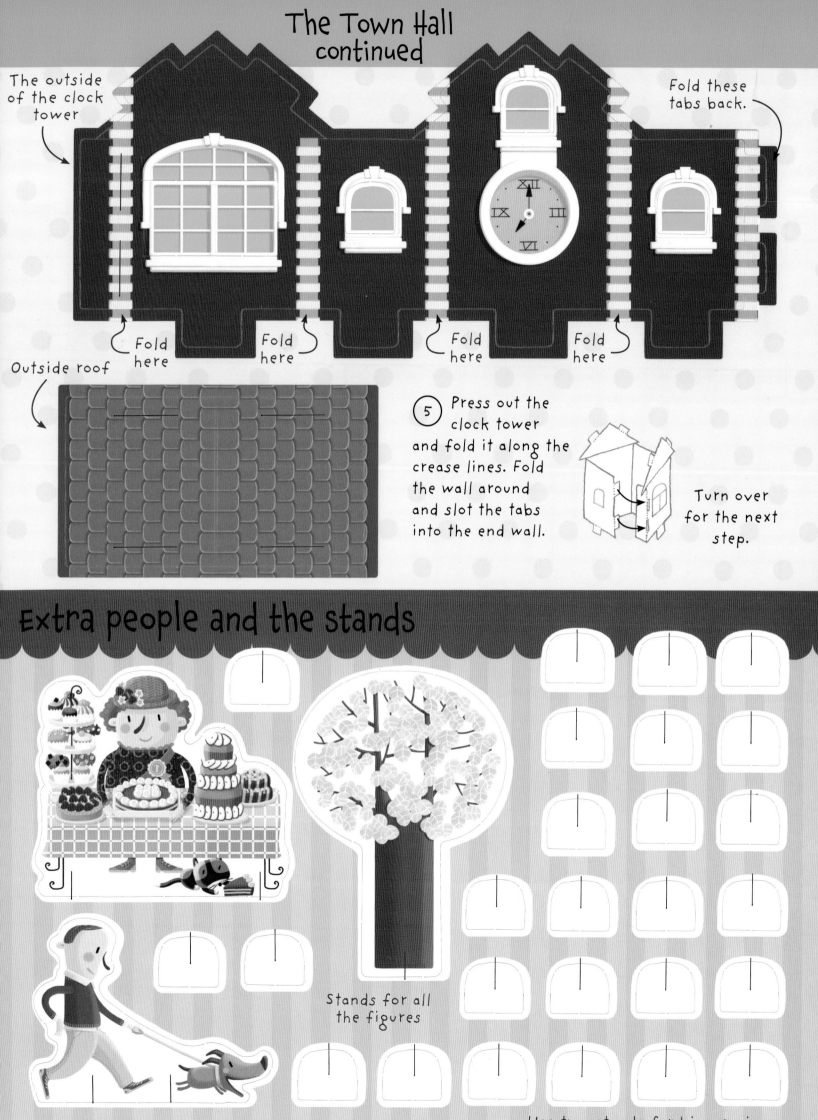

The outside of the clock tower

Fold these tabs back.

Fold here

Fold here

Fold here

Fold here

Outside roof

5. Press out the clock tower and fold it along the crease lines. Fold the wall around and slot the tabs into the end wall.

Turn over for the next step.

Extra people and the stands

Stands for all the figures

Use two stands for bigger pieces.

The inside of the clock tower

Inside roof

6. Press out the roof and fold it along the crease. Slot the roof onto the clock tower. Then, slot the clock tower onto the roof of the Town Hall.

Digital Manipulation by John Russell

First published in 2015 by Usborne Publishing Ltd., Usborne House, 83-85 Saffron Hill,
London ECIN 8RT, England. www.usborne.com Copyright © 2015 Usborne Publishing Ltd. The name
Usborne and the devices 🎈🌐 are Trade Marks of Usborne Publishing Ltd. All rights reserved. No part
of this publication may be reproduced, stored in a retrieval system or transmitted in any form or by
any means, electronic, mechanical, photocopying, recording or otherwise, without the prior
permission of the publisher. Printed in Heshan, Guangdong, China. UKE